Feelings Made Simple

Anxiety

Written by: Alexis O'Neal

ISBN: 9798339574101 (Paperback)

Library of Congress Control Number: 2024923958

All illustrations by: Canva Artificial Intelligence

Self-published by:
Alexis O'Neal (Casa Grande, AZ)

Disclaimer:

This book includes images generated by Artificial Intelligence (AI) sources. While all writing is attributed to the recognized author, the images were exclusively produced by a third-party AI service. According to the specific third party's AI Product Terms, the use of AI-generated images is permitted as long as the author or rights holder clearly communicates the involvement of AI.

It is important to clarify that the author did not modify, alter, design, or create any of the images presented in this book or on the cover, with the exception of the autobiographical image found on the back cover.

Although multiple sources are referenced throughout, all written material was solely crafted by the author. Additional works have been included merely as extra information resources.

Please excuse any grammatical, spelling, punctuation, or citation errors, as this book was entirely composed and reviewed by the author. The primary objective of this book is to convey content and its message rather than to resolve minor imperfections that may exist.

Moreover, please be aware that the author does not possess a professional background nor license in psychology. Given that psychology is a relatively new scientific discipline, information continues to evolve; therefore, the content within this book may change at any time without notice. Neither the author nor any parties involved in the creation of this work can be held accountable for any misinformation, misunderstandings, or negative emotions that may arise from the content provided.

Table of Contents:

Chapter 1: What?

Additional Sources:

Mozafaripour, S. (2024, August 16). *Mental Health Statistics [2024]*. University of St. Augustine for Health Sciences.

Anxiety disorders. (n.d.). National Institute of Mental Health (NIMH). https://www.nimh.nih.gov/health/topics/anxiety-disorders

Anxiety is a part of life. However, **anxiety disorders** (especially the ones we will cover) are consistent and often overwhelming or worsening over time. Symptoms of anxiety disorder can negatively interfere with daily activities such as work, school and relationships.

We will dive into several types of anxiety disorders including generalized anxiety disorder, social anxiety disorder, panic disorder and phobia-related disorders. But first, it is essential to break down what anxiety is, and the symptoms anxiety commonly displays.

Anxiety can manifest in various forms, making it crucial to recognize its multiple facades. Common symptoms can range in presentation, but they are often consistent across different anxiety disorders and include:
-Feeling nervous or restless
-Increased heart rate
-Trouble focusing on anything other than the current worry
-Trouble sleeping
-Difficulty controlling emotions
-Sweating
-Feeling hot
-Shaking/trembling
-Feeling weak or tired
-Breathing rapidly (think of movies showing nervous characters breathing into paper bags)
-Having a sense of impending danger or panic (thinking something bad is going to happen)
-Appearance of paling or reddening skin

-Appearance of a rash or skin discoloration during times of heightened anxiety

Again, while other symptoms may be prevalent or vary from person to person, these are common and the easiest to recognize. Next, we must distinguish anxiety and anxiety disorders. This distinction, though subtle, is significant. Anxiety refers to: a feeling of worry about an upcoming event or an uncertain outcome, and everyone experiences it at some point—whether from preparing for a job interview or confronting a personal fear. For someone without an anxiety disorder, anxiety typically presents manageable (sometimes not even visible) symptoms, and it is usually temporary.

Differentiating between occasional anxiety and a full-blown anxiety disorder can be challenging, especially since many people have only experienced one or the other throughout their lives. Now, this isn't the case for everyone as some people face anxiety disorders after traumatic events or some people's anxiety disorders develop or diminish over time. If you're confused, think of it this way: anxiety is temporary and manageable, anxiety disorders are hindering and frequent. A good way to gauge your anxiety is to simply communicate with your peers or friends and family.

Anxiety disorders are the most common mental health concerns in the United States of America. Over 40 million adults have a diagnosed anxiety disorder (that's 19.1%). Meanwhile, approximately 7% of youth experience anxiety disorders each year. Most people will develop symptoms before the age of 21. This timeframe often coincides with significant life changes, such as starting school, graduating, facing a family divorce, moving out, learning to drive, and navigating numerous college or job applications.

Mental health illnesses such as anxiety disorders are also major concerns among doctors as many who face these issues seek out substances in an irresponsible manner. Statistics show that 33.5% of adults with mental illness also have a substance use disorder. Additionally, 17% of youth with mental illness disorders face major depressive episodes while 12% seriously contemplate suicide. Even in cases where individuals do not recognize their mental illness, suicide remains a pervasive threat across all demographics.

Anxiety disorders are complex conditions that often coexist with various mental health issues, such as depression and substance abuse. This co-occurrence makes treatment difficult to generalize and emphasizes the need for care specific to the individual's symptoms. Furthermore, addressing the stigma surrounding mental health is crucial in encouraging individuals to seek help. Many people are hesitant to seek support due to misconceptions and prejudices regarding anxiety disorders. This will also be mentioned in a later chapter including what the stigma impacts and how it originated.

It's also important to recognize that the experience of anxiety disorders is not identical; it varies significantly from person to person. For some, anxiety is seen through physical symptoms, while others may face cognitive symptoms. This variation shows the need for personalized approaches in both diagnosis and therapy, making sure that each person's unique experience is heard.

This brings up two crucial questions: why do these disorders exist and who do they impact?

Chapter 2:
Who and Why?

Who does anxiety disorders impact? Why does anxiety disorders impact people in different ways? Why are anxiety disorders a thing?

Why does the sun, shine? All of these questions are truly dependent on who answers them. Every single scientist, scholar and professional within their fields have different ideas on each topic and works to prove their theories based on previous research and the missing questions within.

My views may be debated by others within the field of psychology but then again, someone else will debate that person's views too. Who do anxiety disorders impact? Everyone. Everyone can be impacted by an anxiety disorder regardless of whether they have faced a traumatic experience. It truly depends on the person, their environment, their genetics and DNA (the ingredients and recipe), and what some might refer to as, chance.

For context, when I say, "ingredients and recipe", I mean genetics (ingredients) and DNA (recipe). DNA is what each person is made of, and genetics are the small pieces that build your DNA. Therefore, genetics are the ingredients to your DNA recipe! I will also talk about this in a later chapter with a more in-depth explanation.

Nevertheless, there is no pattern or code for who will get an anxiety disorder and who won't. However, there are ways to see who is more likely to experience anxiety disorders compared to their peers. Genetics and DNA play a crucial role in this development of anxiety disorders, intertwined with various environmental and neurobiological factors. Each individual's genetic makeup—the ingredients in their DNA recipe—can predispose them to anxiety disorders, especially if there is a family history of such conditions. Studies indicate that certain genetic traits may make individuals more susceptible to anxiety, yet this interaction is complex and not fully understood.

Anyone can develop an anxiety disorder at any time. There is no set age that it will pop up and there is no set time that you can assume it won't develop. However, statistics indicate a decrease in the prevalence of mental illness among older age groups (people aged 50+), possibly due to their upbringing and prevailing stigma around mental health. It may also be connected to lessened daily stress and improved skills in emotional regulation (such as deep breathing or thinking before acting).

Why do anxiety disorders impact different people in different ways? It just does. Each person is one-of-a-kind and so are their experiences and reactions. It is very difficult to react the **exact** same way since we are all "wired" differently. We all have different genetics and

DNA (ingredients and recipes) making us individuals among our communities. If everyone reacted to anxiety disorders, in the same exact way, we would not understand the variety of these disorders and we would rely on non-personalized, centralized treatment options.

That is the interesting thing about the human body: each body may be made of the same organs and physical brain, but each body has distinctly different DNA (even identical twins don't have identical DNA). Consequently, each person reacts to anxiety in different ways because various factors influence their responses. Not everyone turns to tearful emotions when faced with anxiety; some may express anger while others may choose isolation. Psychology and the study of mental illness is truly dependent on case-by-case analysis and correlation.

Sure, there are studies conducted using sample groups and

medications available for different anxiety disorders, but these approaches tend to address commonalities rather than the individual challenges each person faces. Individual challenges require an additional step of coping mechanisms, communication strategies, medications or therapy resources to help manage everyday life. Science has yet to unlock the full potential of the body and the brain, a mystery that may remain unsolved in our lifetime.

Why are anxiety disorders a thing? No one in the world can answer this question with absolute certainty. Scientists can use scientific findings related to our genetics or our upbringing but there is no definitive reason for the existence of anxiety disorders and why it seems to affect anyone it wants with limited correlation.

While I plan to provide a scientific explanation of causation later in this book, it does not answer this question's deeper meaning of, 'why me' or 'how did this come to be'. Anxiety disorders are simply one of those phenomena we wish didn't exist, but it does. Ultimately, solving this question requires unraveling the mystery of the brain and understanding the full potential of our bodies. Even a simple Google search will often produce a few scientific theories but little more.

While the answers to these questions may not be what you're looking for, they reflect the base answers you will get from many professionals in this field. Although scientific explanations attempt to address these questions, many remain unanswered, perplexing even the most knowledgeable individuals.

Chapter 3: Where and When?

What are some things that cause anxiety disorders? The scientific explanations you may or may not have been waiting for! This is personally one of my favorite chapters as it dives into the answered questions and established facts.

Starting off with what we have previously discussed as causes for anxiety disorders: genetics and DNA. DNA stands for **d**eoxyribo**n**ucleic **a**cid. DNA is a molecule containing the genetics that are unique for every single person (think of our recipe, ingredients example).

Another factor that contributes to anxiety disorders is a chemical imbalance within our brain. Our brains are made of different pieces that all have different jobs. Each piece communicates through messengers called neurotransmitters. A chemical imbalance occurs when either there isn't enough or there are too many neurotransmitters sending messages.

Neurotransmitters have natural chemicals such as dopamine and serotonin. We rely on these chemicals daily to keep our brains and bodies in check. To put it simply, this system connects to the rest of our body's functioning, it is massive and extremely difficult to explain in depth without a professional degree and years of experience.

Dysfunction or chemical imbalances have been linked to various mental illnesses, including, anxiety disorders but some debate this, saying further research needs to be done (I told you, people in science love to debate)!

Another contributor to anxiety disorders stem from previous traumatic experiences a person may have faced in their life such as abuse, neglect, bullying, car accidents, fires etc. Traumatic experiences are anything that produce shocking or dangerous experiences that can affect someone emotionally, physically and mentally.

Finally, another developed factor into what causes anxiety disorders is our environment. While this can tie into trauma and even genetics, our environment makes up a HUGE portion of who we are as a person. Have you ever noticed that some people take off their shoes before entering their homes or pray before meals? These behaviors are influenced by their environment. Your environmental influences are pieces of your life such as social, cultural and physical surroundings that shape your behavior. Anxiety disorders can easily arise from these influences, particularly in today's age of social media.

The overall causes for anxiety disorders are not fully understood but the previously mentioned factors are commonly seen and have been previously linked to anxiety disorders. It is also worth noting that not every individual with an anxiety disorder will fall under every hypothesized factor of development however, they all seem to interact with each other and play a role in each other's evolution.

Psychologists and other mental health professionals can provide further insights and updated information as it is released. All of the information presented in the past three chapters is crucial for understanding the upcoming chapters, where we will explore the most common individual anxiety disorders and their counterparts.

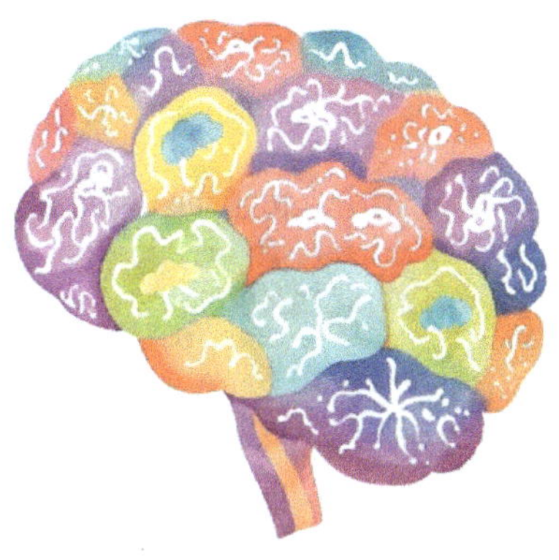

Chapter 4: Generalized Anxiety Disorder

Additional Sources:

Generalized anxiety disorder (GAD). Johns Hopkins Medicine. (2024, April 16). https://shorturl.at/gVB85

Generalized Anxiety Disorder (GAD) is one of the broadest disorders within the realm of anxiety. GAD is often characterized by persistent worrying and the inability to control this worry. But it goes deeper than that, as anyone with an anxiety disorder can tell you.

The differences between Generalized Anxiety Disorder and everyday worry is the intense and consistent worry that alters your daily life. Individuals with GAD often find that their worries are not only relentless but also debilitating. It is common for those with GAD to be diagnosed with additional mental health conditions, further complicating their experiences.

Generalized Anxiety Disorder can stem from a multitude of things ranging from the inability to cope with internal stress (unrealistic expectations, pessimism etc.) to health conditions or even substance abuse.

Generalized Anxiety Disorder has some very common symptoms which tend to make reactions much more intense than what a situation may call for. Some of the more common symptoms are:
- -Trembling
- -Trouble sleeping
- -Headaches
- -Overstimulation
- -Tensing
- -Nausea
- -A lump in your throat
- -Trouble focusing

-Trouble making decisions
-Feeling trapped
-The inability to relax
and much more.

That's the super awesome fun part about healthcare and psychology! This variability makes understanding GAD uniquely challenging, as different individuals exhibit different symptoms and reactions. Thus, healthcare professionals must often rely on educated guesses, particularly in psychology, where visible symptoms are infrequent.

Treating GAD is not a one-size-fits-all type of deal. Treatment can range from medicine to therapy to simply making lifestyle changes. Psychologists and other mental health professionals aim to provide personalized treatment based on your individual needs.

If you find yourself questioning how to recognize GAD or wondering if you've missed underlying signs, know that this is a common oversight.

It can be difficult to notice subtle symptoms, particularly if you lack familiarity with mental health issues. Even those with prior mental health experiences or experience with mental illness may struggle to connect symptoms.

For parents and caregivers, maintaining open lines of communication with teachers, coaches, tutors, or other trusted figures in a loved one's life can be invaluable. These individuals spend substantial time with your loved one and can observe subtle behaviors or changes in reactions to stressors, such as tests or competitions.

Even checking in at the end of every semester and asking the teacher to look out for any signs/symptoms before the school year begins is a great way to stay on top of mental illness and making sure to get the needed support before their anxiety disorder negatively alters their daily life and opportunities.

Generalized Anxiety Disorder can be officially diagnosed and documented in one way, through a healthcare provider. You will never get the help or diagnosis you need and deserve if your healthcare provider is an internet search.

Professionals in this field (namely psychologists, counselors and psychiatrists) have dedicated years to studying the intricacies of mental health in order to offer personalized care. It is essential to seek out a provider with whom you feel comfortable with and can trust.

This principle applies broadly across various mental illnesses and other disorders. It's crucial not to feel embarrassed or guilty when seeking help or asking questions. Every effort to understand and support yourself or someone else is valid and significant.

Chapter 5: Panic Anxiety Disorder

Additional Sources:
Panic disorder: when fear overwhelms. (n.d.).
National Institute of Mental Health
(NIMH). https://www.nimh.nih.gov/health/publicatio
ns/panic-disorder-when-fear-overwhelms

PANIC! Panic Anxiety Disorder (PAD) is a disorder where people have sudden and unexpected panic attacks. These attacks manifest as an overwhelming sense of fear or discomfort, often accompanied by feelings of losing control, even in the absence of real danger or apparent triggers. It is important to note that experiencing a panic attack does not necessarily indicate that a person has PAD or will develop it in the future.

The physical sensations associated with panic attacks can be distressing and debilitating. Individuals may experience:

-Struggle breathing
-Hyperventilating
-Inability to concentrate
-Tingling sensations
-Chest pain
-Increased heart rate
-Dizziness
-Weakness
-Uncontrollable shaking
-Depersonalization

These symptoms create an intense feeling of dread, negativity and frustration. People with panic disorder will typically go out of their way and alter their routines (otherwise known as avoidance behaviors) to avoid having these sudden and unpredictable attacks. Avoidance behaviors are prevalent across many mental illnesses especially anxiety disorders simply because it eliminates or limits the possibility of feeling anxiety symptoms. However, relying on avoidance behaviors can lead to health depletion and they usually cause more harm than good.

Consequently, many individuals develop a pervasive fear of losing control, accompanied by a lingering sense of doom regarding future panic attacks. These attacks can occur anywhere from multiple times a day to a few times a year. PAD often begins in the late teenage years or in early adulthood, making early intervention crucial.

Research indicates that Panic Anxiety Disorder may have a genetic component. Some scholars believe that panic attacks are seen as false alarms within our bodies that are caused by our cortisol (stress level hormones) being too high, too often. This means your body assumes it is in danger even in safe environments and has not had time to relax or reset (think of your electronic devices overheating after you have used them all day without turning them off).

One key characteristic of PAD is the seemingly random nature of panic attacks, which occur with little to no identifiable triggers. Given the elusive origins of PAD, treatment options are currently limited. The best thing to do is to work with a healthcare provider to make sure PAD is not connected to a physical problem. Your provider will then give you resources such as local psychologists, psychiatrists or others to gain a diagnosis.

Current treatment for Panic Anxiety Disorder typically involves psychotherapy and medication.

Medicinal treatment is a very popular method for mental illness. Some effective medications for PAD would be anti-depressants, beta-blockers and anti-anxiety medication. These medicinal interventions have proven beneficial for many individuals grappling with the challenges posed by PAD.

Chapter 6: Social Anxiety Disorder

Additional Sources:
Social anxiety disorder (social phobia) - Symptoms and causes. (n.d.). Mayo Clinic. https://shorturl.at/V8L0R

Social Anxiety Disorder, or SAD, is not simply "sad" or something to be ashamed of; none of these disorders should cause shame. Social Anxiety Disorder, also known as social phobia, manifests when everyday interactions generate anxiety, self-consciousness, and embarrassment due to a fear of being judged or scrutinized by others. This anxiety can easily disrupt everyday life and even lead to impacted relationships at school, work, other activities or daily routines.

Feelings of shyness in public isn't necessarily SAD, particularly in children. Some people are just naturally quiet and prefer to remain reserved in social settings. SAD typically develops in the early to mid-teens, but it can start at any age.

Some of the symptoms of Social Anxiety Disorder include:

-An intense fear of interactions with strangers

-Fear that others will notice your anxiety
-Fear of your physical symptoms showing (blushing, sweating, shaking voice, etc.)
-Avoidance of speaking
-Anxiety in anticipation of an upcoming event
-Self-analysis/criticism of your flaws in social situations
-Hyper-awareness of the people around you
-Expectations of the worst possible outcome during a social event
-Performance anxiety

For children, this may be reflected in tantrums, crying and clinging to parents or refusing to speak. For adults, this can cause panic attacks or worsening symptoms. It is crucial to differentiate between SAD and typical shyness, as the experiences can sometimes appear similar on the surface.

SAD is relatively common yet often mistaken for issues like "stage fright". Avoidance behaviors are also common with SAD. Social scenarios that are otherwise forgotten can cause people with Social Anxiety disorder extreme challenges such as:

-Looking people in the eye
-Starting and maintaining conversations
-Entering a room where people are already present
-Joining something late
-Eating in front of others
-Using a public restroom
-Going up to an employee at a store
-Trying to get a restaurant staff's attention

These everyday experiences may evoke significant anxiety and are often daunting to even think about, which can lead to isolation and limited social exposure. Some notable characters that may have had SAD are

Todd from *Dead Poets Society* and Adrian from *Rocky*.

Social Anxiety Disorder is a serious condition that can be debilitating. Commonly, it is treated through Cognitive Behavioral Therapy (CBT), exposure therapy, medication, and holistic approaches like meditation or journaling.

Diagnosis for this disorder is done through mental health professionals with tests such as a questionnaire, following the criteria listed in the *Diagnostic and Statistical Manual of Mental Disorders* (DSM-5 aka a psychology lifeline) and a series of conversational questions to help mental health professionals gauge the severity and possible disorders that may be impacting you.

Chapter 7: Phobia Anxiety, Substance-Induced Anxiety Disorder

Additional Sources:
Balaram, K., & Marwaha, R. (2023, February 13). *Agoraphobia*. StatPearls - NCBI Bookshelf. https://shorturl.at/gMtd1

Substance/Medication-Induced anxiety disorder. (n.d.). Yale Medicine. https://www.yalemedicine.org/clinical-keywords/substancemedication-induced-anxiety-disorder

Phobia anxiety is considered a type of anxiety disorder. Phobias are fears that people have of specific things such as clowns, spiders and the dark. Everyone has a fear of something, but some people experience such intense fears that it leads to severe reactions, like panic attacks.

People often avoid known triggers and any situation that may involve coming into contact with their phobia. However, this avoidance can risk one's health. For example, nosocomephobia (the fear of hospitals), can lead individuals to avoid seeking medical care or visiting ill loved ones. This phobia, like most likely stems from a traumatic past incident.

Phobias can even make people feel nauseous or panicky when thinking about them. A notable example is Rachel Green from *Friends*, who has a phobia of anything coming near eyeballs. She physically reacts to anything approaching someone's eye and needs to be restrained when she has an eye infection and must use eye drops.

I would argue that Rachel Green had an intense phobia because she refused the doctor's treatment for her eye infection until he hinted at the risk of losing her eye entirely. Throughout this given episode we can also see Rachel react when her friends touch their eyes or use jokes that revolve around eyes.

Regarding phobias, agoraphobia is a significant condition characterized by intense anxiety. It revolves around the fear that arises when someone is in public or in crowded places where escape from harm or access to help is difficult. Individuals with agoraphobia often try to avoid social situations and may experience panic attacks or panic-like symptoms.

Until the DSM-5 (aka a psychology lifeline) was published,

agoraphobia wasn't considered its own disorder and was listed under other anxiety disorders such as PAD or GAD. The key to this diagnosis is that the individual that faces anxiety about being exposed in public spaces makes active attempts to avoid the situations.

Even in the absence of realistic threats, or when surrounded by loved ones in a safe environment, a person with agoraphobia may still experience intense anxiety and panic. Similar to other phobias, this condition is also thought to stem from past trauma or even parental overprotectiveness. There is no physical test to diagnose agoraphobia; instead, an evaluation examines the individual's fear response across various public settings.

Methods of mindfulness-based practices such as stress-reduction or relaxation techniques may help alleviate symptoms. However, medicine and psychotherapy are the main sources of treatment, even though these methods may vary in technique based on the severity of each person. For example, Sheila in *Shameless (US)* had agoraphobia that was so severe that she was unable to leave her house for many years. Her specific case developed during her daughter's childhood and Sheila's belief that the world is an unsafe place. Her phobia was so pronounced that she feared outside germs or dirt entering her home, which may also connect to other anxiety-based disorders. However, phobias do not need to have identifiable causes as some may develop due to learned behaviors or other factors.

Next, we turn to substance-induced anxiety disorder (SIAD). This disorder arises due to the use, dependence, and withdrawal from substances, which can be legal (like alcohol, caffeine, prescription medications) or illegal (hallucinogens, sedatives, opioids).

The anxiety symptoms associated with SIAD emerge during or after substance intoxication or withdrawal, creating a cycle: individuals consume substances to feel good, but once the effects wear off, they feel bad, prompting them to use more to regain those positive feelings.

SIAD has similar symptoms to withdrawal, intoxication and anxiety alike through intense feelings of worry/fear, restlessness, fatigue, difficulty concentrating, irritability and issues sleeping. These symptoms make it difficult for a person to go about their daily life which leads to stress and isolation.

While there is no singular cause for SIAD, it is known that certain substances can trigger anxiety. Additionally, pre-medicating to "manage" existing disorders can intensify symptoms over time, resulting in substance dependence. SIAD exists on a thin line with addiction, and treatment can be quite challenging. Detoxification is typically the starting point for treatment, this occurs when the body is cleansed of all substances, and you begin the withdrawal period (which could be potentially dangerous). Although medication can aid in treating SIAD, psychotherapy, particularly cognitive-behavioral therapy (CBT), is preferred for long-term efficacy.

You may be confused at this point and wonder what the difference is between addiction and SIAD. The difference is time and cause. Addiction requires the increasing of the substance's doses to reach the desired effect (tolerance). This leads to a broader range of behaviors, ongoing patterns of use and persistent issues within daily life.

In contrast, SIAD specifically relates to a substance's effects on an individual's mental state; it can be temporary, and the feelings of anxiety may resolve after use or only emerge during substance consumption. A good example of this is the book, *I'm Dancing as Fast as I Can*, written by Barbara Gordon.

Just because you or a loved one may have been diagnosed with an anxiety disorder, it does not mean that Substance-induced Anxiety Disorder will be developed, nor does it mean addiction will occur. These cases connect to genetic predisposition, personality traits and environmental factors that influence such behaviors. Due to the broad nature of this chapter, I recommend consulting a healthcare provider for guidance and resources to seek a mental health professional.

Chapter 8: Separation Anxiety Disorder, Selective Mutism

Additional Sources:

Separation anxiety disorder - Symptoms and causes. (n.d.). Mayo Clinic

Flaherty, S. C., & Sadler, L. S. (2010). A review of attachment Theory in the context of adolescent Parenting. *Journal of Pediatric Health Care, 25*(2), 114–121

Selective Mutism Association. (2024, October 10). *Home | Selective Mutism Association.* https://www.selectivemutism.org/

Separation anxiety is commonly seen among children especially infants and toddlers, but it can persist well into adult years. Separation anxiety occurs when individuals get anxious or distressed when we are separated from our source of safety and stability. As a young child this was seen when you cried getting dropped off at daycare or crying when someone new held you when you were a baby. Typically, this anxiety diminishes with time, but separation anxiety disorder represents a significant divergence from the norm, characterized by ongoing and intense anxiety.

Attachment theory, developed by John Bowlby and further explored by Mary Ainsworth, proposed that the nature of early relationships with caregivers significantly influences a child's emotional health, particularly in relation to separation anxiety disorder. The theory states that secure attachment formed during childhood can serve as a protective factor against developing separation anxiety, showing the importance of caregivers' responsiveness to children's needs. Ainsworth identified four attachment styles: secure, anxious, avoidant, and disorganized. Each of these styles aim to reflect variations in caregiver interaction and shaping a child's social and emotional development. These categories represent how early experiences form the foundation for later relationships and coping mechanisms, highlighting the critical role caregivers play in building resilience and security in their children.

If the anxiety associated with separation seems more intense, lasts longer than that of peers, impacts daily activities such as school, or includes behavioral issues like panic attacks, it may indicate a transition from general anxiety to an anxiety disorder. Adults and teenagers can also have separation anxiety, and this can develop later in life although it does not occur as often. An example of later occurance at an adult age is in *Finding Nemo.* Nemo's father Marlin faces a variety of anxiety disorders including separation anxiety which is evident when he drops Nemo off for his first day of school and immediately follows Nemo in an anxiety-filled dread after he hears that they go near open water, beyond the reef. Marlin even suggests taking him out of school and trying again in one or two years.

Common symptoms of Separation Anxiety Disorder include:
-Intense distress when thinking about being away from home/loved ones
-Being clingy towards loved ones
-Constant worry about losing loved ones
- Persistent fear of separation due to negative events (kidnapping, etc.)
- Refusal to engage in activities away from home

-Refusing opportunities because they separate you from home/loved ones
-Not wanting to be home alone or somewhere without a loved one close by
-Refusal/reluctance to sleep away from home/loved one
-Anxiety symptoms occurring during or before separation from home or loved one (going on a trip, going to school, etc.)

Separation Anxiety Disorder may manifest with panic attacks and often involves long-term bouts of fear and angst, especially as an events approach. At this stage, separation anxiety is unlikely to resolve on its own without some form of intervention.

This disorder can also strain relationships and lead to "compassion burnout" for loved ones. Relying solely on one person or a small group of people for emotional support may inadvertently cause them emotional pain. Seeing a loved one face such a debilitating disorder is never easy especially when there is no physical injury that can be tended to and fixed.

Consequently, loved ones may feel stranded and helpless in the face of Separation Anxiety Disorder. When they cannot relate to or effectively help, they may experience feelings of irritability, frustration, or sadness.

The causes of separation anxiety are thought to be life stresses or trauma related to separation (divorce, moving, loved one's passing). Genetics may also play a role as well as the individual's home environment. Like most anxiety disorders, Separation Anxiety Disorder can show decent improvement through medication and psychotherapy techniques.

Another inclusion is Selective Mutism. This condition is characterized by an inability to speak in certain situations, particularly social ones. Individuals may communicate freely in comfortable environments but struggle to speak in new or anxiety-inducing settings such as school. Selective mutism often co-occurs with other anxiety disorders such as social anxiety disorder.

This diagnosis is typically seen between the ages of two to four, but it can impact anyone, even into adulthood. Those with this disorder may experience loss of their daily functioning due to their extreme fear of speaking. It is important to note that this fear arises from anxiety rather than a learning disorder or autism. Unlike these conditions, Selective Mutism only occurs in specific settings that trigger anxiety.

Currently, there is no defined cause for selective mutism; however, professionals believe it may be related to social anxiety and avoidant behaviors. Individuals may avoid talking to limit their fears, and over time, this avoidance can become habitual (habit). You may have seen movies or books where one of the characters was unable to speak due to a past traumatic event, but this is different as Selective Mutism has little documented correlation to traumatic events unlike other forms of mutism.

An example of Selective Mutism is Jackie, in *Puff the Magic Dragon.* Jackie is portrayed as a shy boy with Selective Mutism, who meets Puff, the dragon. Through their adventures, Puff helps Jackie confront and ultimately overcome his anxieties, leading to a breakthrough in his ability to communicate.

Chapter 9: Obsessive Compulsive Disorder

Additional Sources:

PANDAS—Questions and answers. (n.d.). National Institute of Mental Health (NIMH). https://shorturl.at/56rW6

Obsessive-Compulsive Disorder. (n.d.). National Institute of Mental Health (NIMH). https://shorturl.at/dKEWh

Obsessive-Compulsive Disorder (OCD) is mistakenly equated with simply being a "clean freak". OCD is a long-term disorder where an individual experiences reoccurring thought (known as obsessions) or engage in repetitive behaviors (known as compulsions) or both. Individuals with OCD experience symptoms that can be time-consuming and cause significant distress, ultimately interfering with their daily lives.

Obsessions are unwanted thoughts, urges, or mental images that provoke anxiety. Common obsessions include:

-Germs/contamination

-Fear of losing control

-Extreme desire to have things in perfect order

-Aggressive thoughts towards others or oneself

-Unwanted or taboo thoughts regarding religion, harm or other

Compulsions are repetitive behaviors the person feels an urge to complete such as:

-Excessive cleaning

-Placing items in a particular order

-Repeatedly checking things

-Compulsively counting

-Prayer

-Repeating words

It is important to understand that OCD is not related to all of the repeated thoughts, rituals or habits you may see someone do.

Those with OCD typically struggle to control their obsessive thoughts or compulsive behaviors, often spending more than an hour each day on these activities. Unlike habits, compulsions do not provide genuine pleasure; instead, they offer only temporary relief from anxiety. This struggle can lead to significant

challenges in daily life. Some individuals with OCD may also exhibit tic disorders, which involve repetitive movements or sounds. Motor tics are sudden, brief and repetitive such as:
> -Eye movement
> -Head/shoulder jerking
> -Shoulder shrugging
> -Facial expressions

Vocal tics are repetitive things like:
> -Throat-clearing
> -Sniffing
> -Grunting

It is common for people with OCD to also be diagnosed with a mood disorder or other anxiety disorders.

The symptoms of OCD may start slowly and may go away for periods of time, or it may worsen for periods of time. During times of stress or grief, symptoms often get worse. Symptoms may also change over time, with age. People with OCD may avoid situations that trigger symptoms or use substances to cope. Many fear the potential consequences of neglecting their compulsive behaviors, such as harm coming to loved ones or the loss of cherished items.

OCD is one of the more recognizable anxiety disorders to see within differing environments especially home or school. Professionals believe genetics and biology play a role in OCD development as those with OCD may have differences in their frontal cortex and subcortical structures of the brain. These areas impact behavior and emotional responses. Some studies also show an association between childhood trauma and OCD symptoms. From my perspective, this correlation may stem from the sense of 'control' (however limited) that OCD provides—an attempt to mitigate the chaos imposed by traumatic experiences. <u>Again, I am not a professional nor am I a licensed</u>

<u>psychologist, so the previous statement was purely opinion.</u>

There is also a noted connection between the sudden onset of OCD and Pediatric Autoimmune Neuropsychiatric Disorders Associated with Streptococcal Infections (PANDAS). PANDAS refers to a group of symptoms, including tics and OCD, that may affect certain children who have previously experienced strep infections. Ongoing research is examining the relationship between PANDAS, tics, and OCD.

OCD is treated through medication, psychotherapy or a combination of both. However, other approaches, such as exposure and response prevention (ERP) therapy, can also be effective. ERP therapy involves gradually exposing individuals to their fears and obsessions while preventing them from engaging in compulsive behaviors. Adhering to a treatment plan is critical, given that Obsessive Compulsive Disorder is a highly structured disorder. A great example of a character with OCD is Emma Pillsbury from *Glee*. She navigates extreme OCD throughout the series that primarily centers around germs and contamination although there are also visuals of systematic counting.

Social media has also become a powerful platform for sharing personal experiences with OCD or other mental illnesses. Users often disclose their diagnoses and daily struggles, providing valuable insights into their realities. One may see videos about patterned counting, negative thoughts or thoughts of punishments if compulsions aren't complete and even people having to redo compulsions if it wasn't done in a way that appeased their anxiety.

Overall, we should not rely on social media to learn about new topics, but it can and has been incredibly useful to gain real-life examples and further our understanding. Take caution when researching and always prioritize scholastic sources.

Chapter 10: Methods

You saw the chapter's title: "Methods." This chapter focuses on the methods used for understanding anxiety disorders, from the diagnostic approaches that doctors utilize to personal stabilization techniques. Professional treatment methods typically used and ways to help those facing anxiety disorders will be in the next chapter so stick with me.

First up is diagnosing. This serves as a recap, but we will probe deeper into how doctors diagnose anxiety disorders, providing a few examples. Keep in mind that this process is subjective and can vary based on the doctor, your individual situation, and other factors; what I outline here is a generalized approach. First, a physical exam may occur. If you're interested in technology, think of this as a troubleshoot. This may include a blood test to rule out any physical issues causing anxiety, such as hypothyroidism (underactive thyroid). During this physical exam, doctors may also examine your medications to check for side effects that might induce anxiety or emotional fluctuations. You might be surprised by how many medications have side effects related to anxiety or depression symptoms. If there is no underlying cause found during the physical exam, the next step would be a psychological evaluation.

During a psychological evaluation, professionals like psychologists, psychiatrists, or counselors will gather detailed information, such as your family history, the duration and severity of your symptoms, whether these symptoms have occurred before (how they were treated if so), and you will likely be asked to complete a questionnaire about your daily feelings and the impact your symptoms have on your life. Professionals should also take your cultural background or home-life into account when looking you're your symptoms, as these factors can influence the presentation of anxiety disorders. Cross- referencing your symptoms and the DSM-5 book is also extremely common when homing in on a diagnosis. Their goal is to find some sort of foundation or initial idea of what you're going through and what it may have originated from.

Once all this information is collected, these professionals (psychologists, psychiatrists, counselors, etc.) may collaborate with your primary care doctor and any other relevant medical professionals to discuss an appropriate and consistent treatment plan. This collaboration ensures that any other current care remains effective and that any new treatments will not interfere.

Next, let's explore self-stabilization methods. These techniques can be used whenever you experience anxiety symptoms and prefer not to rely on others, or if you find yourself in an environment where you are the only one aware of your disorder. They can also be helpful prior to experiencing symptoms, allowing you to limit their full intensity.

Keep in mind, these methods are purely guidelines and as you spend more time managing your disorder, you will find what works best for you. Some techniques may work for you, some may not but you won't know unless you try.

The first method involves numbers, which are popular tools designed to shift your brain's focus and help ground you.

3-3-3: identify 3 objects, identify 3 sounds, move 3 body parts

5-5-5: breathe in for 5 seconds, hold for 5 seconds, exhale for 5 seconds

5-4-3-2-1: identify 5 things you can see, 4 things you can touch, 3 things you can hear, 2 things you can smell and 1 thing you can taste.

All of these are valuable and can help ground you in a private way which can be quite useful especially with overstimulation or social anxiety. The number technique can be used by anyone and can be repeated until you feel calmer. Another popular method is breathing.

Stomach breathing: Focus on your diaphragm (stomach area) while breathing deeply; your stomach should expand and contract with each breath.

Box breathing: slowly exhale through your mouth for 4 seconds, inhale through your nose for 4 seconds, hold your breath for 4 seconds, exhale for 4 seconds, hold your breath for 4 seconds. During this process, concentrate on the air entering and leaving your lungs rather than external distractions. Fun fact: US Navy SEALs use this technique.

Brain breathing (I made up this name, I don't remember what it's called)**:** close your eyes (or fixate on one specific spot), and take deep breaths in and out, focusing solely on your breathing. If your mind drifts to other thoughts, bring your attention back to your breath.

Finally, an effective method is simply, short-term distraction. Whether that means drawing in a notebook, talking to friends/peers, playing games or keeping other senses busy (like fidgeting with a stress toy). Of course, some of these depend on your environment as you can't always go on your phone or talk to your friends.

Some techniques that may also be beneficial include self-talk, countdowns and short-term security items. Self-talk can revolve around reassuring oneself that the anxiety-inducing event will be over soon and that the individual is safe, surrounded by either familiar people or others who are also feeling anxious (this is particularly helpful during tests, interviews, or competitions). Countdowns may help stay aware and in control during longer anxiety-inducing events such as trips. For instance, maintaining a countdown of days before you're able to return home or complete the event. This can give you something to anticipate and seeing the days decrease can help remind you of how quickly time passed. Finally, a short-term security item such as wearing a specific bracelet can serve as a source of comfort and familiarity. While it may not always be the most reliable resource (especially if forgotten or lost), having something familiar can provide comfort, particularly in anxiety-inducing situations.

Ultimately, it comes down to the individual. I have found that many of the strategies presented to me during my initial introduction into anxiety disorder management did not resonate. Over time, I discovered my own effective methods through trial and error, establishing ways to keep them minimal, private, and free of peer distractions. While this is my personal preference, finding what works for you and understanding how it works is crucial, especially given that there is no definitive cure for anxiety disorders. Those living with anxiety often face long-term challenges that cannot always be alleviated through medication alone, so adding self-stabilizing methods will enhance your coping skills.

Chapter 11: Help!

Additional Sources:

Beta blockers. (2023, August 22). Mayo Clinic. https://www.mayoclinic.org/diseases-conditions/high-blood-pressure/in-depth/beta-blockers/art-20044522

Sheffler, Z. M. (2023, May 26). *Antidepressants*. StatPearls [Internet]. https://www.ncbi.nlm.nih.gov/books/NBK538182/

I hope you are all thinking of *"Help!"* by The Beatles. This chapter is all about typical treatment methods and ways to help someone who has anxiety disorder. Again, this is general information and can vary based on your personal situation.

Treatment! The two major forms of treatment that you should at least be familiar with by now are psychotherapy and medication. Psychotherapy is used to teach different ways of reacting to the feelings of your anxiety disorder or other mental illness, this may help alter the physical sensations/reactions. Psychotherapy is often depicted in popular media where patients discuss their feelings to a psychologist while they lay on a couch (this isn't always the case). Another method is exposure therapy which is exactly as it sounds. You are focusing on confronting your fears or beliefs that may trigger panic attacks and in return you build a layer of resilience towards the triggers.

As I previously mentioned, psychotherapy is typically seen as talk therapy. However, psychotherapy can have a variety of treatments such as group talk (Alcoholics Anonymous, support groups etc.) and peer-based support.

The goal of psychotherapy is to unpack issues, understand them and explore options for treatment such as the previously mentioned methods. Psychotherapy addresses issues differently than medication by focusing on cognitive patterns, coping mechanisms, and social/communication skills. While there is a stigma surrounding psychotherapy and mental health in general, it has proven extremely useful and is becoming more accepted every day.

A subset of psychotherapy is Cognitive Behavioral Therapy (CBT). CBT is one of the leading approaches within psychotherapy. It employs research-backed methods to help patients reframe their thoughts and reactions. CBT typically involves efforts to change negative thinking and behavioral patterns. It is conducted in a collaborative manner between the patient and mental health provider. Some examples include using role-playing to prepare for potentially anxiety-inducing interactions, creating a step-by-step plan to face fears rather than avoid them, and recognizing negative thoughts then reevaluating them to be more positive.

Medication is another popular method, and it just so happens to introduce the field of psychiatry. A psychiatrist is a medical doctor within the field of psychiatry who specializes in mental health and has the ability to prescribe medication and provide a range of treatments. The medications prescribed for anxiety disorders do not cure anxiety but help manage the symptoms. For example, rather than feeling anxious 14 times in one day, medication may help reduce that number to 1-2 times per day. There is a multitude of medications available for mental health disorders, especially for the variation of anxiety disorders. It may take a few tries to find the right fit for you, and that is perfectly fine; you want quality, not quantity. Your psychiatrist will have answers to any and all questions regarding medication and common misconceptions related to its use.

Just to help you understand I will list some general medicinal categories you may encounter for anxiety disorders.

Benzodiazepines: Sedatives that help relax muscles and calm the mind by increasing the neurotransmitters associated with happiness (such as serotonin and norepinephrine). These are usually prescribed for short-term use.
Familiar names: Xanax, Valium, Klonopin

Antidepressants: Medications that affect neurotransmitter levels (they work to fix the chemical imbalance). They usually take 4-6 weeks for noticeable effects. There are multiple categories of antidepressants, including monoamine oxidase inhibitors, tricyclic antidepressants, and selective serotonin reuptake inhibitors (SSRIs).

Selective Serotonin Reuptake Inhibitors (SSRIs): a type of antidepressant that increases serotonin levels.

Familiar names: Prozac, Zoloft, Paxil

Beta Blockers: While primarily used to treat heart conditions, they also help relieve physical anxiety symptoms. They work by lowering blood pressure, blocking the effects of adrenaline, widening veins and arteries to increase blood flow. Beta blockers can help manage anxiety before or during anxiety-inducing events, such as a big test or a public speech, making them situational aids.

Familiar name: Propranolol

There are also home treatments to help with anxiety, including changes in diet/exercise, meditation, chamomile tea or supplements, and avoiding substances that may increase anxiety, like caffeine. All of these have been shown to impact daily anxiety positively and are worth trying.

Lastly, here's how to help those who have anxiety disorders. It is crucial to listen and educate yourself on or about these disorders. The last thing someone experiencing heightened anxiety wants is for someone to rush in and draw attention to them when they're just trying to cope. While it's human kindness to help others, it's essential to gauge the situation. Quietly and calmly ask if they need anything, like water or fresh air, or if they want assistance with anything at all. Sometimes, people prefer to stabilize themselves privately. A great example of quiet intervention can be found in season 6, episode 8 of *BoJack Horseman*. Hollyhock is having a social anxiety-based panic attack at a party and rather than draw attention, someone quietly goes up to her and has her try a grounding technique before offering to get fresh air.

Another effective method is to discuss strategies with the person (this method is best used if you know the person well). This conversation gives you insight into what to expect when the person experiences anxiety symptoms. Techniques and helpful methods vary from person to person, but common approaches include talking them through their calming techniques or engaging them in distracting conversation. For example, Perrito helped Puss in Boots through his panic attack in *Puss in Boots: The Last Wish*

If you frequently interact with someone who has an anxiety disorder, it's also a good idea to carry a small amount of their medication or an extra stress toy they use. This gesture can make a significant difference, especially when people cannot access their own items. However, this should only be done with explicit permission, and this is best to do as a guardian, loved one, school nurse, coach or another trusted adult.

Finally, the most important things you can do is to understand, educate yourself and accept the practices of anxiety disorders. Practicing empathy can also be an incredibly helpful skill when attempting to understand anxiety disorders. By practicing empathy, you're putting yourself into the shoes of someone who has an anxiety disorder allowing yourself to experience the compassion and patience needed. Taking the time to understand what anxiety disorders entail can mean the difference between a full-blown isolating episode or the ability to calm down and continue with the day. For example, if someone with social anxiety is facing heightened anxiety, the last thing you want to do is loudly address the issue in front of a group or point out the individual. Context matters. Depending on the person, they may prefer you to go about your day and pay them no mind as they practice self-stabilization. This approach allows them to feel like any other person and provides the environment they need to reset safely. Providing distractions and gradually reintegrating them into conversation without pause can also be beneficial.

Overall, the best advice I can offer is to assess the situation, communicate with the person in advance (if possible), and give them the time and space they need. There are very few ways to know the specifics of someone's anxiety disorder without proper background information, which can be challenging, but communication will make all the difference.

Chapter 12: Nope!

Additional Sources:

Ahad, A. A., Sanchez-Gonzalez, M., & Junquera, P. (2023, May 26). *Understanding and addressing mental health stigma across cultures for improving psychiatric care: A narrative review*. Cureus. https://www.ncbi.nlm.nih.gov/pmc/articles/PMC10220277/

NOPE! It's time for the nitty gritty of anxiety disorders, mental health and psychology as a whole. This chapter focuses on the important topic of what to avoid when interacting with individuals who have anxiety disorders. We'll also discuss the stigma surrounding mental health and the phrases that should be avoided in these conversations. It's important to note that the recommendations provided here are subjective and can vary from person to person.

The stigma associated with mental health and mental illness has been a long-standing issue in psychology, even predating its establishment as a field of study. Stigma is the idea of disgrace or misunderstanding associated with something. Let me say this again, **THE STIGMA ON MENTAL ILLNESS IS HUGE.** In fact, I could write an entire series just discussing this topic and its historical implications.

Alarmingly, a large percentage of those with mental illnesses do not seek help. Many individuals avoid treatment due to fears of being treated differently, perceived as weak, or losing their jobs and relationships. I myself have seen individuals scoff at the idea of mental illness and the field of psychology as a whole. Stigma, prejudice, and discrimination are prevalent within people's view of psychology and mental health, and even in recent times, they continue to affect countless lives. Some people may not even recognize their own negative biases toward mental illness and disabilities. Historically, mental illnesses were often attributed to demonic possession or witchcraft, which forced many individuals to conceal their struggles or not even realize the immense struggles they faced.

In the 1950s and 1960s, deinstitutionalization emerged as a movement aimed at transitioning support from long-term psychiatric facilities to community-based mental health resources. Prior to this shift, individuals could be institutionalized for reasons as trivial as poverty or possessing radical political views. Many of these institutions have dark histories marked by inhumane treatment methods and inadequate patient care. Again, further research into this topic will make a world of difference when understanding the stigma around mental illness especially with the way institutions are portrayed within media.

Research on stigma reveals a troubling paradox: although people may acknowledge the medical involvement of mental health disorders and the necessity for treatment, negative attitudes toward those suffering from mental illness still persist. Stigma can manifest in different ways.

Public stigma involves the negative attitudes that a society may have about mental illness. **Self-stigma** involves the negative attitude including internalized shame that people with mental illness may have. **Structural stigma** involves the governmental and organizational policies that limit opportunities for individuals with mental health issues.

The stigma surrounding mental illness also extends into various cultural contexts. For instance, in some Asian cultures, seeking professional help is often viewed as a disrespect towards values centered around emotional restraint and avoiding shame. Other groups might oppose mental healthcare based on religious beliefs. Particularly for men, there's an added pressure to appear emotionally resilient, further complicating their willingness to seek help thanks to the traditional gender roles portrayed throughout media in the 1940's-1950's. The issue of avoiding help is also notably severe among first responders, healthcare workers, agriculturalists, veterans, and others in high-stress professions. A great example of this is shown by Chris Kyle (portrayed by Bradley Cooper) in *American Sniper*. Chris Kyle experiences PTSD after his time as a Navy SEAL and is seen harboring vivid flashbacks and having aggressive reactions to everyday occurrences. While PTSD is no longer considered an anxiety disorder, it is still a useful example in this instance when recognizing the disregard and lacking public acceptance for mental illness.

What we urgently require is increased awareness, acceptance, and education regarding mental health issues. Awareness entails understanding the profound impact that anxiety disorders and other mental health conditions can have on individuals. Acceptance involves recognizing the validity of mental health issues and the necessity for treatment. Finally, education about the nuances of mental illness—especially within the broad spectrum of anxiety—is essential. There is no reason to shy away from discussions about anxiety or mental illness; these topics deserve open dialogue and recognition. It is not a taboo conversation, it is a field of growing, internationally recognized healthcare and science!

In summary, stigma leads to delayed treatment, lower quality of life, and harmful stereotypes. Mental illnesses and anxiety disorders are as real as any physical ailment—even if they remain invisible. No one chooses to develop an anxiety disorder or any other mental health issue that impacts daily life. My final word to this topic is to ignore the stigma (easier said than done for some) and do what is best for your personal health.

Next, let's discuss what you should avoid doing or saying. To summarize, it's important not to draw attention to someone who is experiencing heightened anxiety. Additionally, never shame someone or make them feel inferior for having emotions that differ from your own. A simple comment like "Really? You're still worried about that?" can be damaging. Individuals with anxiety disorders often overthink to the extent of losing sleep or feeling nauseated over issues that are long forgotten by others.

You may not always know what is troubling them, and they may struggle to pinpoint the source of their distress themselves. It's wise to avoid dismissive phrases such as "just relax," "calm down," "you're overreacting," or "don't worry." If someone with an anxiety disorder could simply stop worrying, they would; it's much more complex than that, and such remarks can lead to feelings of alienation.

The tone of voice and body language you present can significantly impact a person with anxiety. Those with anxiety disorders are often adept at reading nonverbal cues and subtleties in body language that others might overlook. Therefore, even minor gestures, like a shoulder slump, can carry more weight than intended. While it's not always possible to control your initial reactions, it's valuable to remain mindful of how even a sigh could tip the scales between someone's isolation or self-stabilization.

Additionally, offering unsolicited advice is generally unwelcome—whether from pregnant women, chefs, teenagers, or those on the receiving end of random anxiety suggestions (I recognize the irony, but if you opened this book, I trust you were seeking information).

Acknowledging someone's level of comfort regarding their anxiety disorder is vital and relates to respecting boundaries. For example, if John Doe prefers to keep his personal diagnosis private, it's inappropriate to disclose his General Anxiety Disorder diagnosis to a group even if he shared such information to you prior. Respect their choice to share such information at their own discretion.

It's also crucial to avoid overwhelming someone with questions or attempts towards potential solutions for their anxiety. For example, pushing someone to confront their fears without proper preparation or aid can worsen their symptoms and progress made.

It's also important not to allow your frustration to become a source of tension; dealing with anxiety is inherently tough, and adding anger into the mix only complicates matters further. Experiencing heightened anxiety while facing someone's irritation about your uncontrollable emotions can be incredibly difficult. While frustration is understandable, allowing it to take over will not benefit either party and will likely worsen the situation.

When it comes to physical contact for comfort, preferences can vary widely. For some, physical touch may heighten anxiety rather than alleviate it, while others find solace in emotional support animals, weighted items, or compression techniques.

A noteworthy study of compression comes from Dr. Temple Grandin's research within the agricultural field. Dr. Grandin invented a squeeze machine designed to provide deep pressure therapy to herself during moments of overstimulation and anxiety. This 'squeeze machine' was inspired by cattle squeeze chutes used by ranchers to handle livestock calmly during branding and vaccinations. Dr. Grandin's creation led to a paper and a study conducted with her peers that demonstrated the effectiveness of compression for many individuals. Variations of Dr. Grandin's squeeze machine exist today as valuable tools for compression-based support.

If you are dealing with an anxiety disorder, this chapter still resonates with you. There's no need to diminish your own experiences for something beyond your control. Comparing your struggles to others, even those facing more significant challenges, is unproductive. Your emotions and struggles are valid. You are doing your best with what you have, taking necessary steps to manage your anxiety disorder. Remember that struggles are not linear; some days will be more challenging than others but turning to harmful practices or substances won't resolve those difficulties; in fact, it will likely increase your struggles. It's essential to remember that support is available, and it takes strength to seek help. Anxiety disorders, manifest differently for each individual, with varying severity, symptoms, and coping strategies. Meaning, you are piecing together your one-of-a-kind puzzle, one that has not been solved for you.

There are many resources available to support both yourself and your interactions with those who have anxiety disorders; please don't overlook them.

Chapter 13: Overview

This chapter is an overview of everything you have read about, resources to help guide your own research and a simplification of medical terms that have been used throughout the book!

Chapter 1: Anxiety is a common part of life, but anxiety disorders can be overwhelming and persistent, impacting daily activities. There are various types, including generalized anxiety disorder, social anxiety disorder, panic disorder, and phobias. While temporary anxiety is manageable, anxiety disorders are chronic and debilitating. Anxiety can lead to serious consequences, including substance abuse and suicidal thoughts, prompting a need for understanding and support.

Chapter 2: Anxiety disorders impact everyone, influenced by genetics, environment, and individual circumstances. Each person's unique genetic makeup leads to varying responses and experiences with anxiety, making it impossible to generalize treatment. Factors like gender and family history can increase susceptibility, but anyone can develop these disorders at any time. Despite research into causes and treatments, the fundamental reason for the existence of anxiety disorders remains uncertain, highlighting the complexity of mental health.

Chapter 3: Anxiety disorders can stem from various causes, including genetics, chemical imbalances, traumatic experiences, and environmental influences. Genetic predisposition plays a role, as DNA uniquely shapes each individual. Despite ongoing debates in the scientific community, these factors are widely recognized as contributing to anxiety disorders.

Chapter 4: Generalized Anxiety Disorder is a complex condition that requires individualized attention and treatment. Recognizing symptoms and seeking professional help can lead to improved mental health/quality of life. Through shared understanding and open communication, we can foster supportive environments that prioritize mental well-being for everyone.

Chapter 5: Panic Anxiety Disorder (PAD) is characterized by sudden, unexpected panic attacks that induce intense fear and physical discomfort without clear triggers.

Chapter 6: Social Anxiety Disorder (SAD), often misunderstood, involves intense fear and anxiety in social interactions due to a fear of judgment. Diagnosis is facilitated through discussions with mental health professionals based on criteria from the DSM-5.

Chapter 7: This chapter discusses various phobias and anxiety disorders, emphasizing that while everyone has fears, some can be so intense they lead to panic attacks. Agoraphobia, characterized by fear in crowded or public spaces, was only recognized as its own disorder in the DSM-5. The chapter also covers substance-induced anxiety disorder (SIAD), caused by substance use, dependence, and withdrawal.

Chapter 8: This chapter discusses separation anxiety and selective mutism. It highlights the difference between typical separation fears and separation anxiety disorder, which involves intense, lasting distress impacting daily life. Selective mutism occurs when individuals can speak freely in familiar settings but struggle in anxiety-inducing situations.

Chapter 9: Obsessive Compulsive Disorder (OCD) is a complex, long-term condition characterized by persistent unwanted thoughts (obsessions) and repetitive behaviors (compulsions). Symptoms can vary in severity and may worsen during stressful periods. This chapter highlights the importance of adhering to prescribed plans.

Chapter 10: This chapter discusses methods related to anxiety disorders, focusing on diagnosis and self-stabilization techniques. It outlines the diagnostic process. The chapter also introduces self-stabilization methods suitable for personal use. Ultimately, it highlights the importance of finding individualized strategies for coping with chronic anxiety, as there is no definitive cure.

Chapter 11: This chapter discusses treatment methods for anxiety disorders, focusing on psychotherapy and medication. Psychotherapy, including CBT (cognitive behavioral therapy), helps develop coping strategies through collaboration. Medication, prescribed by psychiatrists, can help manage symptoms without curing anxiety. Home treatments are also beneficial. To assist those with anxiety, it's crucial to listen, respect, and support them while understanding their individual situations. Communication is key in providing effective help.

Chapter 12: This chapter covers the stigma surrounding mental health, and what not to say or do for those affected. Stigmas, deeply rooted in history, deter many from seeking help due to fears of judgment and discrimination. The text emphasizes the importance of understanding that mental illnesses are legitimate and valid, much like physical ailments. It outlines unhelpful phrases and behaviors which can exacerbate anxiety. The chapter encourages empathy, highlighting available resources for support and communication.

Terms Simplified:

Alienation - the feeling that you have no connection with people around you

Avoidant behaviors - actions people use to distract themselves from distressing situations

Chemical Imbalance - too much or too little of a substance meant to help your body

Cognitive- relating to conscious activity such as thinking or remembering

Coping mechanisms/techniques - tools people use to help themselves in difficult situations (typically emotional)

Cortisol - stress hormone

Dependence - relying on or being controlled by someone or something

Depersonalization- feeling detached from body or surroundings

Diagnosis - the identification of an illness or issue

Detoxification - steps meant to manage withdrawal

Dopamine - neurotransmitter chemical that makes you feel satisfied and motivated

Deinstitutionalization - the release of individuals from institutional care into the community

Emotional regulation - ability to manage and respond to emotional situations

Fatigue - feelings of exhaustion and lack of energy

Genetic predisposition - a higher chance of developing a disease based on genetics

Hyperthyroidism - too much activity of the thyroid gland, causing quick heartbeat

Hyperventilation - rapid, shallow breathing

Isolation - the state of being or feeling alone

Impairment - function or condition being weakened

Influxes - an entry of large numbers
Longevity - long existence or life
Neurobiological- study of the biology of the nervous system
Overstimulation - being overwhelmed by more noise/sensations/activity than you can process
Sample groups - a small group meant to portray a larger population (in studies)
Serotonin - neurotransmitter chemical that makes you feel happy, calm and focused
STEM - the field of science, technology, engineering, and math
Self-stabilization - taking yourself from a feeling of unease to a more positive, calm feeling
Studies - learning something by investigating, reading, reflection (like an experiment)
Subset - a smaller part of a large group
Tolerance - when the body gets used to a substance, so more is needed now than in the past
Traumatic Experiences - anything that produces a shocking or dangerous experience that can affect someone
Triggers - something specific attached to someone's trauma that causes them to react negatively (ex: loud noises)
Underlying - hidden, not obvious
Withdrawal - the symptoms someone has when they suddenly stop the use of an addictive substance

If you are interested in researching and finding more information on anxiety disorders or psychology in general, I recommend looking into the following resources:

www.apa.org
American Psychological Association

https://www.nimh.nih.gov
National Institute of Mental Health

https://www.mayoclinic.org/diseases-conditions
Mayo Clinic

Websites that end in .edu or .gov are also reputable. Anything academic that I have referenced within this book is also from reputable sources ranging from academic journals to designated associations based solely on those specific topics.

Sources Mentioned:

Separation anxiety disorder - Symptoms and causes. (n.d.). Mayo Clinic. https://www.mayoclinic.org/diseases-conditions/separation-anxiety-disorder/symptoms-causes/syc-20377455#:~:text=Separation%20anxiety%20disorder%20is%20diagnosed,from%20home%20or%20loved%20ones

Selective Mutism Association. (2024, October 10). *Home | Selective Mutism Association*. https://www.selectivemutism.org/

Balaram, K., & Marwaha, R. (2023, February 13). *Agoraphobia*. StatPearls - NCBI Bookshelf. https://www.ncbi.nlm.nih.gov/books/NBK554387/#:~:text=Agoraphobia%20is%20the%20anxiety%20that,may%20occur%20in%20these%20situations.

Substance/Medication-Induced anxiety disorder. (n.d.). Yale Medicine. https://www.yalemedicine.org/clinical-keywords/substancemedication-induced-anxiety-disorder

Social anxiety disorder (social phobia) - Symptoms and causes. (n.d.). Mayo Clinic. https://www.mayoclinic.org/diseases-conditions/social-anxiety-disorder/symptoms-causes/syc-20353561

Flaherty, S. C., & Sadler, L. S. (2010). A review of attachment Theory in the context of adolescent Parenting. *Journal of Pediatric Health Care, 25*(2), 114–121. https://doi.org/10.1016/j.pedhc.2010.02.005

Mozafaripour, S. (2024, August 16). *Mental Health Statistics [2024]*. University of St. Augustine for Health Sciences.

Panic disorder: when fear overwhelms. (n.d.). National Institute of Mental Health

(NIMH). https://www.nimh.nih.gov/health/publications/pan ic-disorder-when-fear-overwhelms

Generalized anxiety disorder (GAD). Johns Hopkins Medicine. (2024, April 16). https://www.hopkinsmedicine.org/health/conditions-and-diseases/generalized-anxiety-disorder#:~:text=What%20is%20generalized%20anxiety%20disorder,for%20at%20least%206%20months.

PANDAS—Questions and answers. (n.d.). National Institute of Mental Health (NIMH). https://www.nimh.nih.gov/health/publications/pan das#:~:text=PANDAS%20is%20short%20for%20Pediatric, strep%20throat%20or%20scarlet%20fever.

Obsessive-Compulsive Disorder. (n.d.). National Institute of Mental Health (NIMH). https://www.nimh.nih.gov/health/topics/obsessive -compulsive-disorder-ocd#:~:text=Obsessive%2Dcompulsive%20disorder%20(O CD),or%20interfere%20with%20daily%20life.

Beta blockers. (2023, August 22). Mayo Clinic. https://www.mayoclinic.org/diseases-conditions/high-blood-pressure/in-depth/beta-blockers/art-20044522

Sheffler, Z. M. (2023, May 26). *Antidepressants*. StatPearls [Internet]. https://www.ncbi.nlm.nih.gov/books/NBK538182/

Ahad, A. A., Sanchez-Gonzalez, M., & Junquera, P. (2023, May 26). *Understanding and addressing mental health stigma across cultures for improving psychiatric care: A narrative review*. Cureus. https://www.ncbi.nlm.nih.gov/pmc/articles/PMC10220277/

Anxiety disorders. (n.d.). National Institute of Mental Health

(NIMH). https://www.nimh.nih.gov/health/topics/anxiety-disorders

Friends
Created by: David Crane, Marta Kauffman (1994-2004)

Puff the Magic Dragon
Directors: Charles Swenson, Fred Wolf (1978)

Shameless (US)
Adapted by: Paul Abbott, John Wells (2011-2021)

Dead Poets Society
Director: Peter Weir (1989)

Rocky
Director: John G. Avildsen (1976)

Glee
Created by: Ian Brennan, Brad Falchuk, Ryan Murphy
(2009-2015)

I'm Dancing as Fast as I Can
Author: Barbara Gordon (1979)

Diagnostic and Statistical Manual of Mental Disorders,
Fifth Edition
Author: American Psychiatric Association (2022)

Help!
The Beatles (1965)

Puss in Boots: The Last Wish
Directors: Joel Crawford, Januel Mercado (2022)

American Sniper
Director: Clint Eastwood (2014)

Temple Grandin Ph.D.

American academic, professor, best-selling author, animal
behaviorist, autism self-advocate, advocate for the humane
treatment of livestock for slaughter

Temple Grandin
Director: Mick Jackson (2010)

Finding Nemo
Directors: Andrew Stanton and Lee Unkrich (2003)

BoJack Horseman
S6E8: A Quick One, While He's Away (2019)
Created by: Raphael Bob-Waksburg (2014)